HOW TO FIX
YOUR MARRIAGE

BY

WALE ODEYALE

HOW TO FIX YOUR MARRIAGE BY WALE ODEYALE

First Edition: 2021 Lagos – Nigeria

All Scripture references in this book are from the King James version of the Holy Bible unless otherwise stated.

ISBN: 9798517830784

Published by
AGAPE LOVE MARRIAGE FOUNDATION (ALMF)
Lagos, Nigeria

abidemielshaddai@gmail.com | olaideodeyale@yahoo.com
Telephone: +234-8033193560; +234-8037194890

Printed by
www.smartblyno.com; +234 803 309 0137

CONTENTS

This book, **HOW TO FIX YOUR MARRIAGE**, is dedicated to the glory of the Triune God – the Owner of life and Distributor of Grace for the strength and inspiration to write this book.

It is also dedicated to my wonderful wife of 30 years and still counting, my Angel of inestimable value, Pastor Mrs. Olaide Odeyale and my four children, Tomilola, Tobiloba, Tosin and Temi for their immense support.

This book is also dedicated to all men and women in the ministry of building the marriage institution.

APPRECIATION

I want to sincerely appreciate the Almighty God for supplying the inspiration to write this book, in contribution to building the oldest institution in the world (the marriage institution).

I am grateful to my wonderful wife of 30 years and still counting, my Angel of inestimable value, Pastor (Mrs.) Olaide Odeyale and my four children, Tomilola, Tobiloba, Tosin and Temi for their immense support.

I appreciate the grace of God upon the life and ministry of my father-in-the- Lord, Pastor Enoch Adejare Adeboye for giving me the platform to function effectively in ministry. I thank my Pastor-in-Charge of RCCG Lagos Province 12, Pastor Timothy Olaniyan and his amiable wife Pastor (Mrs.) Aanuoluwani Olaniyan for the opportunity to serve God in the Province.

I also thank his Assistants, Pastor Sade Paul and Pastor Fred Odekhian together with their wives. I thank my Pastor friends and their wives namely Pastor & Mrs Anthony Akomolafe, Pastor & Mrs Bode Oyadiran, Pastor & Mrs Shem Oluwagbayi, and Pastor & Mrs Samuel Asamaige for their support and encouragement and for lifting my hands in ministry. I also thank all Pastors in RCCG Lagos Province 12 and their wives.

I sincerely thank my two daughters, Tomilola and Temilola for taking time to type the entire manuscripts of this book. The Lord will bless you for your support and send timely support to you in Jesus name amen.

I thank Deaconess Nkechi Ejiogu for helping me proof-read the typed pages of this book to ensure it is error free. God bless you for a good job. I appreciate all the Ministers, workers, men and women of RCCG Lights' Chapel for being there for me and my family. The Lord will not forget any of you in Jesus name amen.

Pastor Wale Odeyale

May 2021

Marriage is very fragile. It is as fragile as a crate of egg. Many people who refuse to carry marriage as a delicate item have since found out they have lost out and their marriage is in jeopardy.

Marriage is an essential part of God's arrangement and He does not want couples to be careless in handling their marriages. Couples need to fix their marriage lest they become victims of broken marriage.

No effort should be spared to fix a marriage because once a marriage is broken, the couple and their children are in a big fix. The husband is disabled, the wife is worn out while the children are done for. In short, when there is a break in the flow of marriage water, everyone within the reach of the relationship is in a big dilemma.

For a marriage to be fixed and for it to stand the test of time, couples must work on certain areas of their relationship.

One of such is the use of the tongue which is of great essence in marriage. The tongue is the medium of communication so it is of great essence. However as important as the tongue is, it has to be tamed or else it would create a great problem for the marriage. The tongue could become what is referred to as 'banana peel' in that as smooth as it is to use, it could be a source of great discomfort in marriage.

The wife should not compete with the husband on who can abuse the most. Her words should be seasoned to promote love from her husband and her communication should be well packaged with plenty of appreciation, with a view to getting the best out of her husband. In fact, her presentation to a large extent determines how the husband will view her and do her bidding.

For the husband, he needs to be swift to hear and slow to speak. As a matter of fact, he should not speak as a man when he is angry. When provoked, he should take a walk out instead of remaining at the scene to continue hearing the unpalatable from the wife, refusal to leave the scene could also provoke a fight and the tendency to beat up the wife. Once that happens, there would be a breach in that marriage relationship.

Couples have been brought into marriage by God with the instrumentation of men and women that provided counselling and they must both be alive to fulfil their marriage vows.

Another area that must be worked on is the area of sex. The couple must not deny each other sex. They are both to enjoy the liberty of sex in a lawful marriage. When sex is enjoyed in marriage, there is an undeniable peace and harmony. When sex is an issue in a marriage, trouble is bound to develop and grow and that does not do anyone any good. If couples enjoy their sex life in marriage, they both will be under severe judgment if they go out and commit adultery. The word of God has enough warning against adultery in marriage. There is no excuse for adultery and God is going to judge every act of adultery.

Another area that must be critically worked on to fix your marriage is to address without delay what a man or a woman wants in marriage. This poser is one key thing that sustains marriage. For the man, he wants to be respected, honoured and cared for by his wife. For the woman, she wants to be loved, pampered and celebrated as a toast by her husband.

Marriage is a tonic for good life. Marriage is both an eye opener and a door opener. An eye opener as it enables the couple to be abreast of new roles vested on them by marriage. It is also a door opener as it has the potential to open new chapters in the life of the couple. In fact, the society sees the married man as a responsible man while the woman is seen as a favoured person woman.

Head or tail, marriage is the beginning and the end of great developments and no effort should be spared at getting the best out of it. Marriage must be guided and no stone should be left unturned to ensure it does not end up in divorce.

Pastor Wale Odeyale
May 2021

x

CHAPTER ONE

Regulating Your Marriage Speedometre

Marriage is very fragile and it must be handled by the two people involved (husband and wife) as a crate of egg that must not be broken.

So many people handle marriage like a carton of Indomie noodles forgetting that when the carton shielding the packets of Indomie falls, the carton absorbs the fall so the content is preserved from injury. That is not the case of the crate of egg. Once it comes in contact with any other unfriendly object, it breaks as there is no tailor or any gum or glue that can fix it together except by divine intervention. A broken relationship before marriage is okay but once marriage is entered into, the husband and wife must carry it like a crate of egg that must not fall down or be allowed to drop suddenly.

When a marriage gets broken, so many things get broken with it. Husband and wife become disabled, dis-orientated and remain in-capacitated while their children remain unsettled, uncared for and are at the mercy of a care-free or wayward society.

For any marriage to go far in life, there is a dire need for the speedometer of such marriage to be put under check and be firmly controlled.

In Proverbs 18 verse 21, the Bible talks about the tongue and the need to guide its usage before it sets the whole atmosphere ablaze.

The tongue is the speedometer of the body. It is a two-edged sword processing life and death. The tongue is a big pit to the one not careful in his or her conducts. In I Peter 3 verse 10, we are told that he that loves life and desires to see good days should tame his tongue (speedometer).

In marriage, the wrong use of the tongue has pushed couples out of wedlock and they are today separated. The tongue, though small, has very devastating effects. For you to nurture your marriage, you must put your speedometer in great check. Caution must not be thrown unto the winds by not controlling the tongue.

The tongue is the major part of verbal communication and so should be well guided lest it leads marriage into a tight corner. Ephesians 4 verse 29 confirms the power of communication. Husband and wife should apply wisdom in the usage of their tongues to protect their marriage.

As a wife, never be pushed to the corner of lambasting your husband because of what he is going through at a particular time. Remember, that a man is short does not make him a boy, your tongue should be used in talking to your husband with respect and dignity – Matthew 5 verse 37. Proverbs 15 verse 13 talks about the heart of merriment that comes through the tongue.

The wife must talk to the husband with honour he deserves as the head of the family – Ephesians 5 verse 23. When the husband is properly addressed, he is bound to release some virtue unto the wife. You cannot blame a man for not being of help to you as a wife when you are always insulting or casting aspersions on him without end.

As a wife, your husband should be your star and should not be washed down through abuse or molestation. A wife calling the husband 'a good for nothing husband' before the children can never get fulfilment in marriage. She needs wisdom in the usage of her tongue - Proverbs 12 verse 18. Every wife needs to brittle her tongue - Proverbs 13 verse 3. She should not take her husband for granted. She should grant her husband access to her heart through good and seasoned communication by the use of her tongue.

For the husband, he should be swift to hear, slow to speak and slow to wrath - James 1 verse 19. He should be careful what he says to the wife.

His tongue must not be caustic - Proverbs 14 verse 3. He needs to be meek in his speech to his wife. There is a way you say sorry and you mean it and there is a way you say the same 'sorry o-o-o' and it turns to mockery. Your speech should not be damaging but comforting, full of grace and highly encouraging.

Be careful as a husband of what you say when angry, it is better not to speak out of anger as it can be very costly - Proverbs 16 verse 27.

As a husband, take interest in fixing your marriage by regulating your speedometer, you must not be a wireless organ or a busy body but be a real man - Proverbs 10 verse 32. Also, you must carry grace as a husband and such grace is a cover for your family hence the need to be careful what you say - Ecclesiastes 10 verse 12. Your words as a husband and father of your children must be comforting to your spouse and your children - Job 4 verse 4. Caring words and words of consolation should proceed from your lips.

As you speak as a husband and father, God has given you the tongue as a learned - Isaiah 50 verse 4, so speak with great understanding and wisdom like the tongue of Solomon will be deposited unto you in Jesus name.

As husband and wife, speaking pleasant words to one another is good to the relationship. Such words are pleasant as honeycomb, sweet to the soul and health to the bones - Proverbs 16 verse 24.

To guide your tongue as couples, the principle of not speaking when angry is very important. Couples must not make a statement in anger to each other - Proverbs 10 verse 19. No one speaks damnation to himself so why do you want your spouse to be damned by the utterances of your tongue? - Proverbs 17 verse 27. To enjoy their marriage, couples need to keep their tongues so as to stay clear of any trouble – Proverbs 21 verse 23.

Couples must make their speech as comforting as possible to each other. Their speech should always be with grace, seasoned with salt, that they may know how they ought to answer every person – Colossians 4 verse 6.

Couples should be careful what they say as God is witness between them.

CHAPTER TWO

Flee Adultery

As we navigate the end time blow and the hardship it brings, Jesus foretold this season – Matthew 24 verse 12.

As the love of many is beginning to wax old. In fact, some couples love is fading out and as a result adultery and fornication have become the order of the day, other forms of immortality have also increased over time. Today, we see unprecedented immoral behaviours, husband openly displaying infidelity towards his wife and wife doing same to her husband. In the face of overwhelming hardship of life, there is need to flee adultery and all that is tied to it.

The word of God has enough timely warning against adultery in Exodus 20 verse 14 and Leviticus 20 verse10 – both warned against adultery. What then is adultery?

- It is unfaithfulness to one's partner.

- It is preference for another person instead of one's spouse.

- It is selling or giving your soul out to someone else apart from your spouse.

- It is giving consideration to someone else.

- It is the longing or willingness to be with someone else.

- It is preference for another person's view or opinion constantly against that of your spouse.

- It is lack of patience or ability to bear with your spouse while you can tolerate others.

- It is preference to confide in another person instead of your spouse.

- It is finding the company of another person good enough instead of that of your spouse.

- It is feeling at home with a person while being at war with your spouse.

- It is willingness to tolerate someone's mistake but not willing to tolerate that of your spouse.

- Adultery is an act, it is when you are secretly lusting after the opposite sex while your spouse is irritating you.

Adultery in summary is your failing to love your spouse as ordered by God.

Every husband or wife can easily overcome adultery by doing the following:

- By renewing your love for each other in line with the marriage vows before the altar.

- By wanting to be with your spouse all the time.

- By renewing your affection towards your spouse on a regular basis.

- By guiding yourself with the principle that your spouse is the best thing that ever happened to you and thereby sparing your soul – Proverbs 6 verse 32.

- By never contemplating selling what God has given you in your spouse free of charge.

- By not contemplating taking another person into your bosom no matter your level of challenge – Matthew 5 verses 27 and 32; Luke 16 verse18. There is an adage that says when a man decides to eat from two sides of the pot, he should prepare for diarrhea. Do not eat around. Refuse to form company with other women or men aside your spouse.

- By submitting to your spouse no matter how bad his situation may be. Submission is a gift a woman should pray to God for. Your husband is not a slave, do not address him as one. He is your head while you as a wife is the neck. God created the wife as a help meet, fit for the husband and not a headache – Genesis 2 verse18.

- To overcome adultery, the wife must release her body to her own husband. No matter the pressure, no other person should cross her. No matter how nice, gentle or caring another man might be, no other man must cross over her. Her marital vow must not suffer any loss due to adultery.

- As a man, no matter how beautiful another woman may look, never contemplate laying your hands on her. If she is looking pretty and well laid out, spend time on your wife too. Give her some encouragement to work on her body, her clothes and her psychology and you will see her transformed. Someone said if you see a grass green on the field, someone is wetting it. Your wife is your grass, wet her very well and her field will be green and lovely to behold. It is a great and an unpardonable abomination to lie down on a woman who is not your wife. The same goes for a woman who allows a man who has not paid dowry on her to allow such to lie on her.

As a woman, adultery is a great sin. Even if you have enough reason or evidence against your spouse, do not try to retaliate by going the same route. Instead report him to a person who can call him to order. Two wrongs do not make a right. Remember your children are your future and no sacrifice is too much for their sake. Even if you are the bread winner and you think your husband is not worth being given your body as a reward, it is not just enough to go into adultery.

Adultery is a great sin that brings God's anger to those in it. Couples must understand that there is no excuse under which God will permit adultery. No matter the situation or what you are going through, go to your Pastor. Be careful who you share your issues with. We recommend your Pastor as your spiritual head. Most people you are talking with about your marital issues might even mislead you and end up benefitting or taking you for granted based on your situation. Some of these so-called confidants or counsellors you are complaining to, are actually jealous and envious of your marital status.

Rather than speaking to such, call on your Pastor (spiritual father or mother) and he or she will prayerfully counsel you and support you for amicable resolution.

Even when you think all is failing after speaking to your Pastor, you can pray to God about your marriage. God established marriage (Genesis 2 verse 18) and He is still the

Principal and Chief Architect of marriage. God is never tired of His children. The Bible calls Him the present help in time of trouble – Psalms 46 verse 1. No matter how stressed or stretched your marriage becomes, nothing takes God unaware and you can be sure, He is always willing to sort His children out.

Marriage is very important before God and His verdict on marriage is still as relevant as ever. That verdict is found in Malachi 2 verses 15 and16. The Lord will help you!

Colossians 3:13-14

Forbearing one another, and forgiving one another, if any man have a quarrel against any: even as Christ forgave you, so also do ye.

14 And above all these things put on charity, which is the bond of perfectness.

CHAPTER THREE

What Does A Man/Woman Want In Marriage

Marriage is an amazing experience between a man and a woman to the admiration of the whole world. It exists when a man and a woman decide to come together and live together to the exclusion of the whole world. No wonder Genesis 2 verse 24 recommends that husband and wife should leave their past livelihood and cleave to each other and become one flesh.

This coming together was also buttressed in Ephesians 5 verses 31 and 32 and the Bible described it as a mystery. Husband and wife must totally leave their past, cleave to each other and not be distracted whatsoever in the journey towards marital bliss.

The two that has become one must operate fully in unity to ward off strange objects against their joyful marriage. There must be no sentiments in the war against anyone the devil might want to use against the success of their marriage. They must do away with every ego or sense of pride as such could be counter-productive and terminate their hope for a great marital experience.

To be able to address the issues, above husband and wife must have a clear understanding of what they want from each other to boost their marriage and make it an everlasting enjoyment to the glory of God.

Now to the wife, what does her husband want? What are the expectations of a husband from his wife?

The husband of any wife wants to be served and reckoned with. There was the case of a woman who contacted an herbalist to report that her husband does not eat her food. The herbalist, who became a Christian later narrated this story, he said he asked the woman to come back the next day for a concoction to be put in the husband's soup.

The next day, the woman came quite early and the herbalist gave her the so-called love mixture. The woman collected the mixture swiftly gave the herbalist some money and rushed home. The herbalist asked her to treat her husband well before giving him the food to eat and she must also stay around him when eating the food. The woman carried out the herbalist's instructions. She prepared the food and laid the table and requested the husband to eat the food having garnished the soup with the mixture from the herbalist. The husband who has never been well treated like that decided to eat the food and he was promptly served with water to step down the food by the wife. She cleared the table and said thank you to the husband for eating her food. The husband thereafter started coming back home early and peace was restored back to the home.

This woman went back to appreciate the herbalist to collect more mixture and subsequently rewarded the herbalist. This was on for a while before the herbalist repented, gave his life to Christ and counselled the woman that all her husband needed were proper care, attention and service. He confessed all he put in the mixture is simply condiments women used to spice soup and it was not a love medicine as the woman had thought.

As a wife, you need to give your husband proper service and the needed attention. Remember if he goes to the eatery, he is treated like a King and he gets prompt service, so when he comes back home, don't toss his food at him like a dog.

The husband also wants his wife to always massage his ego as the head. He does not enjoy being talked down at like a houseboy. Even when the wife is the temporary bread winner, the man still wants to be treated as one and that makes him fulfilled no matter his psychological state. Men enjoy being celebrated and more so they want that from their wife. A woman that knows how to celebrate her husband before the children and even in public will no doubt get the best out of the marriage. Such women tend to have their wishes established rather than being turned down.

Wives who celebrate their husbands are actually the ones in charge in the home. If your complaint is that your husband does not listen to you, please use the therapy of celebrating your husband and see him making a total 'U-turn' towards your aspiration and desire for a successful or fulfilling marriage.

Another thing a man wants from the wife is total respect. He wants his opinion to count and not be rubbished. Even when he is talking nonsense, he does not want the wife to shun him openly as that deflates his ego, makes him agitated and when that happens his reaction is bound to be negative.

A man also wants to be regarded as number one even though he is not on top of his game. He wants to be reverenced and adored. The thinking of man is that after God, he comes next and he does not expect less from his wife. In Genesis 18 verse 12, Sarah referred to Abraham as 'my lord'. Every man is elated when the wife reverences him. You reverencing other people outside while treating him with disdain at home will not solve your problem in the marriage.

Finally, a man wants his wife to submit to him totally in line with Ephesians 5 verse 22. He wants to call the shots and the wife concurs, he wants her to hear his voice and the wife says 'okay my dear', he wants to tell the wife 'this is where we are going' and she says 'God will help us'. Instead of using the last statement (God will help us), most women always want to proof a point that 'I know more than you'. No man will take this even if the wife is taller, or more knowledgeable or richer than him.

Men grow annoyed and are irritated with their wives when they are compared with another man. No matter how deficient or poor a man might be, he does not enjoy being compared to another man as one better than him. No man enjoys his wife seemingly preferring another man over him. This is a very dangerous area and no man wants to be subjected to it.

Another thing that affects men in marriage is infidelity on the part of their wife. A man can commit suicide if another man takes advantage of his wife. No matter his state, no man wants another man to 'farm' in his farmland. The ego of man will not allow him see his wife being handled by another man. He will rather die than to be so treated.

Another key thing that upsets a man and his character or approach to credible marriage is denial of sex. A man is seriously agitated when the wife denies him sex. When a man is sexually fulfilled, he tends to do so well in other spheres of life. A man denied sex by the spouse could become very brutal, irritated or could even become a stammerer. Such men could even become very aggrieved that they end up nagging.

If women can work on these critical areas and adhere properly, they will experience marital bliss and their homes will become heaven here on earth.

Now what does a wife want in her husband?

The first thing a wife wants from her husband is total love in line with Ephesians 5 verse 25. She wants her husband to display high sense of love towards her, to make her head swell as a woman in the midst of many women. When a woman is loved, she is on top of her world. She is both fulfilled and feels in charge. A wife also enjoys being preferred. She is elated if she gets picked from the crowd of women.

Another thing that gives a wife fulfilment in marriage is the ability of her husband to care for her. She wants a husband that will massage her body when she feels down. She wants a husband that will rub her back when there appears to be an ache. She wants a husband that knows the pin code to her body mechanism not one that does not care for her at all.

Every wife wants to be in charge of certain areas of the marriage if not all. They want to dictate what to eat, what material of clothes to pick, what outfit to wear to outings, etc. The husband must reach some compromise in this area to prevent chaos and constant friction in the home.

A wife also wants to be pampered as a toast by her husband. The husband must pamper her as the honey of his marriage and must be so treated all through the marriage. Another word for being pampered is to be spoilt by her husband which makes her so appreciated.

Every wife wants to be given the opportunity to build her home and be the chief organizer of the home. Women assert this authority as they are naturally endowed by God to have eyes for beauty. Men should reach a compromise on this to avert regular quarrels.

Women get annoyed when they are neglected by their husbands. Nothing gets a wife more irritated than making her second eleven or on the reserve bench. Some husbands who are ardent football supporters tend to lose their wives as they concentrate so much on watching their darling football clubs while neglecting their wives. This is a very unfortunate act and should be addressed accordingly.

She also hates to be insulted or molested openly before relatives, friends, children, etc. Such will make a woman lose her sense of belonging and such can even ruin the marriage.

There are clear areas of distinction between a man and a woman. In the area of sex, every husband should understand that a wife loves romance while he loves sex. The 'process' for the husband is quick and it advances easily while that of the wife is gradual, systematic and procedural. While the husband loves to spend money, the wife is wired to save money for the rainy day.

To overcome the opposite positions, husband and wife must address one another, in trying to maintain their God-given positions without any competition.

Proverbs 5:18-19

Let thy fountain be blessed: and rejoice with the wife of thy youth.

Let her be as the loving hind and pleasant roe; let her breasts satisfy thee at all times; and be thou ravished always with her love.

CHAPTER FOUR

Marriage as a Divine Harvest

Marriage is a tonic for good life. In fact, when a man or woman gets married, life receives a new lease. Marriage is an exalted position. Marriage is both an eye opener and also a door opener; if marriage is gotten right, it brings better things like salvation.

However, for marriage to be sweet, it must be done with the right partner. Marriage is indeed a glimpse of heaven here on earth, provided the two people becoming one are together in every sense of the word.

Marriage with the right person is Divine Harvest. In Genesis 2 verses 18, 20 through 24, Adam received Eve with so much joy. That joy brought a quick revelation to Adam and he spoke the word of authority declaring Eve as his bone of bones. This is clearly an indication that when you marry the right spouse, joy is constant.

Marriage also opens fresh doors of progress and opportunities. From experience, my own marriage in 1991 was a floodgate of opportunities. My wife got a job in a bank the week we got married. I also got a super-sonic job in a choice place the following month after my marriage.

Immediately we settled in, both my wife and I began to feel the new touch of favour and today, I can say boldly that marriage is full of miraculous occurrences - in fact, it is a season of harvest without bounds. Any marriage where the husband and wife marry right is bound to go places and that is the story of my marriage.

Marriage brings comfort - Genesis 24 verse 67. It is the beginning of paradise and it eliminates shame - Genesis 2 verse 25.

Marriage is a Divine Harvest basically because a wife is a good thing - Proverbs 18 verse 22. A husband is a diamond and a lovely thing. This is why you should be positive about your spouse. Never express any negative mindset about your spouse because your spouse is a perfect gift from God and He expects you to receive him or her with gratitude to God.

God expects the man to enjoy the wife of his youth – Proverbs 5 verse 18. The husband is expected to dress his wife as a beautiful garden and is not permitted to admire or lust after other women. His spouse must be his only source of satisfaction. No other person can do what your spouse can do positively and even if he or she has some negative tendencies, such should be considered and converted as manure for some positive developments. Absolute love in the relationship should overtake all offences or negative tendencies.

Ecclesiastes 9 verse 9 says "Live joyfully with the wife whom thou lovest all the days of the life of thy vanity". Here God sentenced man and woman with everlasting enjoyment in marriage.

When marriage is on the scene, every tendency for loneliness must depart without ambiguity.

Marriage as ordained by God is meant to kill and terminate boredom totally and absolutely – Genesis 2 verse 18.

Marriage brings complete enjoyment, and this explains why when a man gets married, his diet is bound to improve. His food would no longer be that of a bachelor and he begins to flourish as a responsible person in the community of reasonable or honourable people.

Husband and wife are expected to live in total independence from every interference – Matthew 19 verses 4 and 5. For marriage to be successful, the couple is expected to have a good time for each other without any third-party influence or unnecessary interference like asking about what kind of food is cooked, how much money is at the disposal of the wife for home maintenance or upkeep and so on.

The couple must be allowed to make mistakes until they form an undeniable alliance meant to work for their benefit. God expects husband and wife to be united together in all things according to Ephesians 5 verse 31. While the husband is open to the wife in financial affairs, at running the home, the wife must be frugal or prudent, so the family does not go into debt. In short, the wife must not be a financial burden to the husband by pursuing extravagant things like "aso-ebi" or "owambe" outfits, latest shoes, bags, etc.

Both husband and wife are to be considerate and be one in all things. Marriage has so many benefits which cannot be totally explained on the pages of books no matter the number or volume of chapters. Marriage is indeed a Divine harvest. It is like 'a pot of soup' of great celebration, a lasting enjoyment and an everlasting joy beyond description.

OTHER BOOKS BY THE SAME AUTHOR

- FAITH: THE UNIVERSAL CURRENCY

- THE COLOURFUL MARRIAGE

- LOVE IS A VERB

- MARRIAGE WITHOUT TEARS

- THE MARRIAGE SYLLABUS

- HOPE FOR TROUBLED MARRIAGE

- HOW TO FIX YOUR MARRIAGE

- BE CAREFUL BEFORE YOU SAY "I DO"

- TO LEAVE AND TO CLEAVE

For further enquiries, counselling, talks on
marriage and prayers:

Please call or write:

+ 234 803 319 3560

+ 234 803 719 4890

E-mail address:

abidemielshaddai@gmail.com
olaideodeyale@yahoo.com

www.ingramcontent.com/pod-product-compliance
Lightning Source LLC
Chambersburg PA
CBHW071500150726
48000CB00006B/2640